A VISUAL OLD TESTAMENT

BOOK ONE:

FROM ABRAHAM TO DANIEL

Writ

A. G. PATSTON

THE RELIGIOUS EDUCATION PRESS

(A Division of Pergamon Press)

HENNOCK ROAD EXETER EX2 8RP

First published 1961
Twelfth Impression 1980

Printed in Great Britain by A. Wheaton & Co. Ltd, Exeter

ISBN 0 08 006132 X (non net)
ISBN 0 08 017667 4 (net)

BEFORE YOU BEGIN!

IN the Old Testament there are thirty-nine books—books of history, of law, and even of poetry. In them you will find many stories telling you about great people who lived long ago. This book should help you to understand how the stories about them are really linked together, and to take you, step by step, through the history of the Jewish people.

Only the outlines of the stories are given to you, so try to read more about them for yourself in the Bible—there is a reference on each page to help you to find the place in the Old Testament. The pictures, maps, and diagrams are here to help you to 'see' the story more clearly, and to show you the sequence of events, or how one happening followed another.

Try to make your notebook as attractive as possible. You can copy or trace the diagrams or, better still, draw your own pictures to illustrate the stories. There are many ideas to help you to make your notebook interesting.

Perhaps, as you read on, you will be able to understand how God taught the Hebrews about Himself and how the past of long ago is linked with the Christian faith of today.

This book forms one of a comprehensive series, all in the same style and format, covering the Old Testament, the New Testament and the history of the Christian Church:

A VISUAL BIBLE

A VISUAL OLD TESTAMENT, Book One: From Abraham to Daniel. Includes twenty-one pictorial summaries of the outstanding Old Testament characters such as Abraham, Jacob, Joseph, Moses, Joshua, Gideon, Elijah and others.

A VISUAL OLD TESTAMENT, Book Two: Abraham to Division of the Kingdom. This covers the beginnings of Hebrew history going back into the time of legend and myth and moving into the early history of the Kingdom of Israel up to the death of Solomon.

A VISUAL OLD TESTAMENT, Book Three: From the Division of the Kingdom. This book covers the story of the history of the Hebrew nation from the time of Solomon through the period of the prophets and up to the end of the Old Testament period.

A VISUAL NEW TESTAMENT, Book One: Jesus, Mighty in Word and Deed. Twenty-one stories and twenty-one diagrams of the life of our Lord, covering his birth, early ministry, his teaching, his miracles, and his mighty acts and deeds.

A VISUAL NEW TESTAMENT, Book Two: Saviour of the World, continuing the life and teaching of Jesus from his tragic journey to Jerusalem and his crucifixion on Calvary, and his resurrection and triumphal ascension.

A VISUAL NEW TESTAMENT, Book Three: All that Jesus began—the founding of the Christian Church by the Apostles under the power of the Holy Spirit, including the work of Peter, Philip and others.

CONTENTS

ABRAHAM—THE FOUNDER OF A NATION

ABRAHAM, whose name means the father of a multitude, was chosen by God to lead the Israelites. The Jews have always thought of him as the founder of their nation and the tales they told about him were gathered together into the Book of Genesis.

Abraham lived in the town of Ur in southern Babylonia about 2000 years before the birth of Christ. He and his father, Terah, were rich men with many servants, sheep and cattle. The people of Ur worshipped, in great temples, the sun god and the moon god.

Abraham wanted to worship only the one true God and he and his wife Sarah and his father and relations went northward to Haran. Here Terah died and Abraham, obeying the command of God, went to Canaan with Sarah and his nephew Lot. From there they were driven, by famine, to Egypt where they grew very rich with flocks, herds and followers.

On their return to Bethel, the flocks of Abraham and Lot grew so large that it was difficult to get water for them and their shepherds quarrelled over the wells. Abraham knew they must part and generously gave Lot the first choice of pasture. Lot chose the fertile plains of the Jordan and Abraham was left with the barren rocks of Judaea.

After some years, great trouble came to Lot and, in a fierce battle, he was carried off as a slave. Abraham generously went to his rescue and not only set him free, but regained his flocks and herds for him.

FOR YOUR NOTEBOOK

1. Draw a picture of the tents and wells with sheep and shepherds.
2. Read Genesis **13.** 1-17.
3. Write a few sentences imagining that you are Abraham offering Lot the choice of pastures.

ABRAHAM

The people worshipped in great temples the sun and moon gods

ABRAHAM AND LOT JOURNEYED INTO THE DESERT

THEIR SHEPHERDS QUARREL OVER THE WELLS

ABRAHAM KNEW THEY MUST PART

WEST

Abraham goes to the barren rocks of Judaea

HE GIVES LOT THE FIRST CHOICE

EAST

Lot chooses the fertile plains of the Jordan

ISAAC—THE SON OF ABRAHAM

ABRAHAM and Sarah grew very old and were anxious to have a son. According to the custom of the East, Abraham took a second wife called Hagar, and a child was born who was called Ishmael.

Later, God told Abraham that Sarah would have a child and the promise was fulfilled with the birth of Isaac. Sarah became jealous of Hagar and Ishmael because she feared for Isaac's inheritance and she persuaded Abraham to send them away into the wilderness.

The descendants of Ishmael became a great nation — the Arabs.

Whilst Isaac was still a young boy, God tested Abraham by commanding him to go to the top of a mountain and to offer Isaac as a sacrifice. Abraham did as he was told, but, as he was about to kill the boy God spoke to him again.

'Lay not thy hand upon the boy, for now I know that thou fearest God.' As he looked up, Abraham saw a ram held fast by its horns amongst the briars and this he offered as a sacrifice to God in the place of Isaac.

Not many years after, Sarah died and Abraham became anxious for the marriage of Isaac. He sent his trusted servant Eliezer back to Haran to find a wife for Isaac.

Eliezer returned with Rebekah and she and Isaac were married. Twin sons were born to them, Esau and Jacob.

The tribe of Abraham learned how to grow crops (Genesis **26.** 12).

FOR YOUR NOTEBOOK

1. Read the story of the sacrifice in Genesis **22.** 1-14.
2. Draw a picture of Eliezer meeting Rebekah outside the gates of Haran.
3. Make a model of a well.

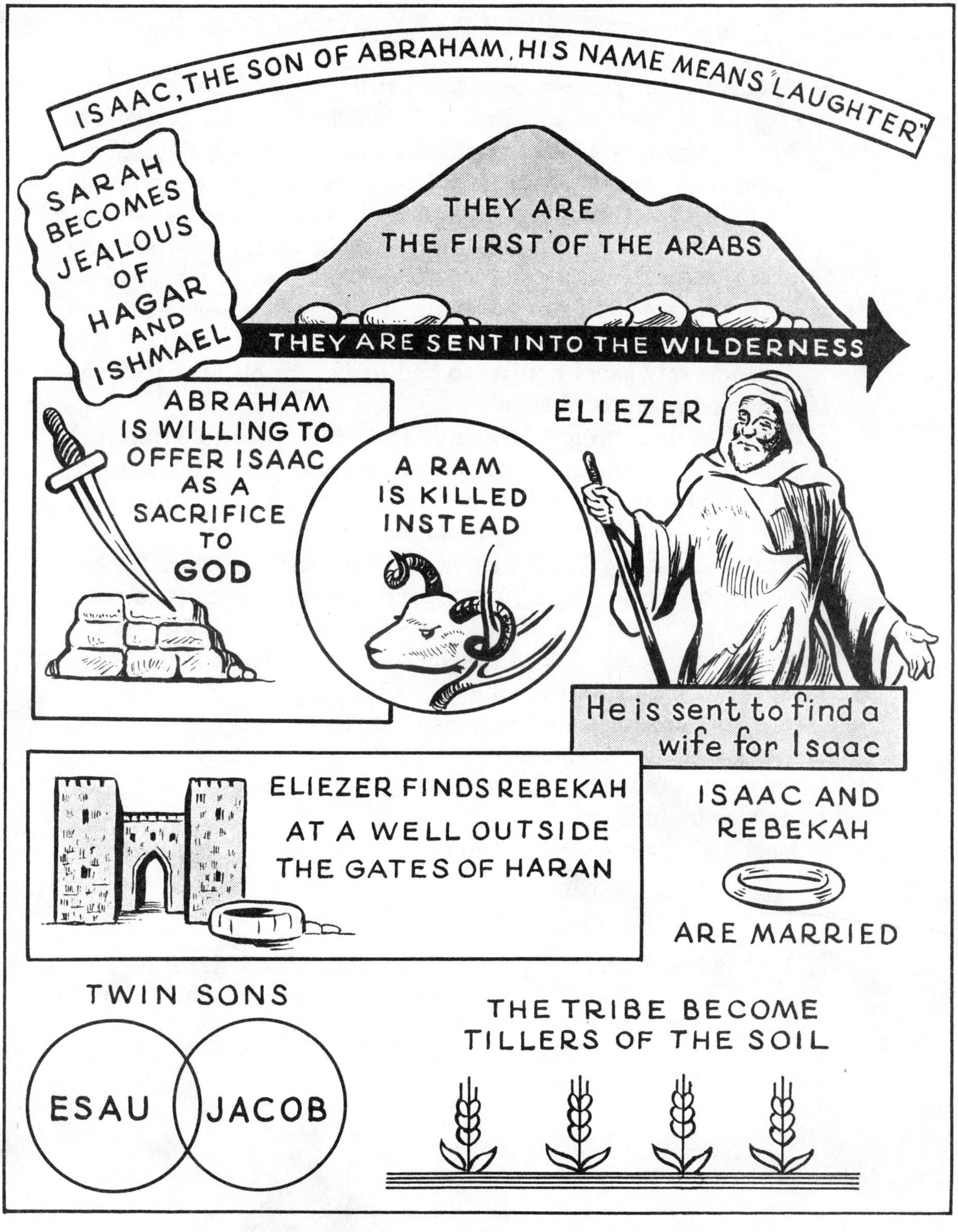

ISAAC, THE SON OF ABRAHAM, HIS NAME MEANS "LAUGHTER"

SARAH BECOMES JEALOUS OF HAGAR AND ISHMAEL

THEY ARE THE FIRST OF THE ARABS

THEY ARE SENT INTO THE WILDERNESS

ABRAHAM IS WILLING TO OFFER ISAAC AS A SACRIFICE TO GOD

A RAM IS KILLED INSTEAD

ELIEZER

He is sent to find a wife for Isaac

ELIEZER FINDS REBEKAH AT A WELL OUTSIDE THE GATES OF HARAN

ISAAC AND REBEKAH ARE MARRIED

TWIN SONS

ESAU

JACOB

THE TRIBE BECOME TILLERS OF THE SOIL

JACOB—SUPPLANTER AND PRINCE

ISAAC, the peacemaker, settled at the place of the seven wells called Beersheba. His two sons differed greatly. Esau, the first born, was the daring hunter whilst Jacob was the dreamer and shepherd. On one occasion, Esau, famished with hunger, sold his birthright in exchange for a meal his brother had prepared.

When Isaac was very old and nearly blind, Jacob, dressed in his brother's clothes and with kid skins on his hands and neck, deceived his father by pretending to be Esau. In this way he obtained what was his brother's by right.

Esau was very angry and Jacob had to flee for his life. Rebekah sent him to her brother Laban.

It was on this journey, at Bethel, that God spoke to Jacob in a vision. Jacob dreamed that he saw angels ascending and descending a ladder which stretched from heaven to earth. In this vision God blessed Jacob and renewed His promises.

When Jacob arrived at Haran, he met his uncle's daughter Rachel. Struck by her beauty, he offered to work for seven years (as a shepherd for Laban) so that he could marry her. However, Laban tricked him into marrying his elder daughter Leah, and Jacob had to work another seven years for the hand of Rachel.

Jacob decided to return to Canaan. On that journey he was again blessed by God and named Israel, the Prince of God.

On his return, Esau forgave him and the families settled down peacefully together.

Jacob's children were the founders of the twelve tribes of Israel.

FOR YOUR NOTEBOOK

1. Write a few sentences explaining how Jacob tricked Esau.
2. Read Genesis **28.** 12-15 and draw a picture of Jacob's dream.
3. As Jacob tricked Esau so Laban tricked Jacob. How was this?

JACOB

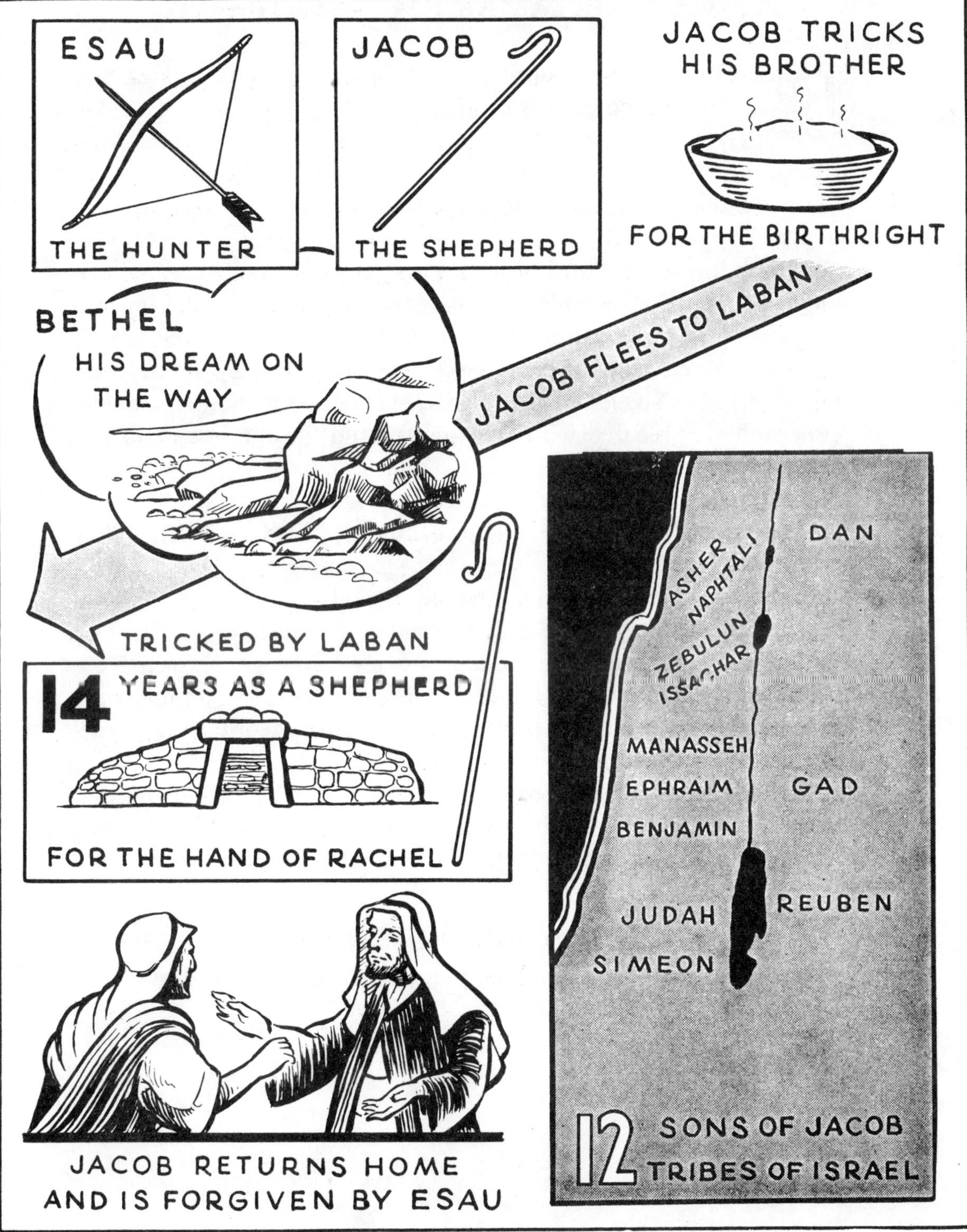
ESAU
THE HUNTER
JACOB
THE SHEPHERD
JACOB TRICKS HIS BROTHER
FOR THE BIRTHRIGHT
JACOB FLEES TO LABAN
BETHEL
HIS DREAM ON THE WAY
TRICKED BY LABAN
14 YEARS AS A SHEPHERD
FOR THE HAND OF RACHEL
DAN
ASHER
NAPHTALI
ZEBULUN
ISSACHAR
MANASSEH
EPHRAIM
GAD
BENJAMIN
REUBEN
JUDAH
SIMEON
12 SONS OF JACOB
TRIBES OF ISRAEL
JACOB RETURNS HOME AND IS FORGIVEN BY ESAU

JOSEPH—DREAMER AND STATESMAN

JOSEPH was the favourite son of Jacob, and his father gave him a beautiful coat. His brothers were jealous of him. One day they threw him into a pit and then sold him to passing merchants.

The merchants journeyed to Egypt where Joseph was sold as a slave to Potiphar, but was later thrown into prison.

Pharaoh, the king, heard of his success at interpreting dreams and Joseph was sent for to explain a strange dream in which the king had seen seven lean cows eating seven fat cows. Joseph told the king it meant that seven years of plenty would be followed by seven years of famine and he suggested that a great store of corn should be made.

Pharaoh was pleased with this answer and he put Joseph in full charge of the scheme.

During the famine, which spread to Canaan, Joseph's brothers came to Egypt to buy corn. Joseph recognised his brothers but they had no idea who he was.

He decided to test them. First he sent them back to fetch Benjamin, the youngest, and kept Simeon as a hostage. When they returned with Benjamin he accused them of stealing his silver goblet which he himself had caused to be hidden in Benjamin's sack. Finally he made himself known to his brothers and forgave them for their cruel treatment years before.

Pharaoh heard of this reunion and, being grateful to Joseph, invited Jacob and his family to the green fields of Goshen. Thus they came to Egypt where they lived happily for many years.

FOR YOUR NOTEBOOK

1. Draw Joseph's long-sleeved or many-coloured coat or draw Arab merchants with their camels.
2. Read about Pharaoh's dream (Genesis **41.** 1-8) and describe it in your own words.

JOSEPH

JOSEPH, THE FAVOURITE SON OF JACOB
HE IS GIVEN A LONG-SLEEVED OR MANY COLOURED COAT
HIS BROTHERS ARE JEALOUS OF HIM
THEY THROW HIM INTO A WELL
HE IS SOLD AS A SLAVE
AND TAKEN INTO EGYPT
CORN IN EGYPT
7 FAT YEARS
7 LEAN YEARS
JOSEPH FORETELLS PHARAOH'S DREAM
AND BECOMES RULER OF ALL EGYPT
HIS BROTHERS COME TO EGYPT
SIMEON IS KEPT AS A HOSTAGE
THE BROTHERS RETURN
A SILVER GOBLET IS FOUND IN BENJAMIN'S SACK
JOSEPH REVEALS HIMSELF
JACOB AND HIS FAMILY SETTLE IN THE LAND OF GOSHEN
The Great Sea
GOSHEN
EGYPT
Red Sea
R. Nile

MOSES—THE LAW-GIVER

AFTER the death of Joseph, the Israelites (or Hebrews) became very numerous in Egypt. The king (Rameses II) became afraid of their numbers and tried to crush them by making them slaves and giving them all sorts of hard labour.

In spite of this, the Israelites increased and the king decided on the cruel method of drowning all Hebrew boys as soon as they were born.

At this time a Hebrew boy was born and his mother, to save him from death, hid him in a cradle amongst the reeds of the river Nile. There the daughter of the king found him and decided to adopt him. She took him to the palace and named him Moses which means 'saved from the waters'.

Moses grew up in the palace and was taught the wisdom of the Egyptians, but he could not forget that he was a Hebrew.

One day, when visiting Goshen, he saw an Egyptian cruelly beating a Hebrew slave. Filled with anger, he killed the Egyptian and buried him in the sand. Knowing that his life was now in danger, he fled into the wilderness. There he became a shepherd to Jethro and married Jethro's daughter, Zipporah.

Forty years passed and the sufferings of the Israelites in Egypt became worse. Then God appeared to Moses in a burning bush and gave him the command to return to Egypt and lead his people to freedom.

FOR YOUR NOTEBOOK

1. Read Exodus **2.** 3-10.
2. Make a model, from raffia, of a Moses basket, or act the scene of the princess finding 'Moses in the bulrushes'.
3. Read Exodus **3.** 1-6, and copy verse 6 in your best handwriting.

MOSES

EXODUS
THE ISRAELITES HAD BECOME SLAVES IN EGYPT
THEY MADE BRICKS AND CARRIED WATER
PHARAOH ORDERS THE DEATH OF ALL HEBREW BOY BABIES
A BABY BOY IS HIDDEN AMONGST THE REEDS
FOUND BY A PRINCESS THE BABY IS CALLED MOSES AND BROUGHT UP IN THE PALACE
MOSES KILLS AN EGYPTIAN AND FLEES TO THE WILDERNESS
HE BECOMES JETHRO'S SHEPHERD AND MARRIES ZIPPORAH
MOSES SEES THE BURNING BUSH AND HEARS THE COMMAND OF GOD
Go unto Pharaoh and bring forth my people, the children of Israel, out of Egypt.
Exodus 3

THE EXODUS

MOSES returned to Egypt and, with his brother Aaron as spokesman, asked Pharaoh to let the Israelites go. Pharaoh refused because the Israelites were so useful as slaves.

Many terrible plagues then overtook the Egyptians. The water became undrinkable, frogs and flies and locusts swarmed over the land, cattle died and great storms damaged the crops. The Israelites were untouched by these plagues.

Finally, one night, the eldest child in every Egyptian home died and Pharaoh, afraid of more disasters, agreed to let the Israelites leave Egypt.

Moses at once gathered the people together and they prepared for the journey. Before departing they ate a hasty meal. This was the first 'Feast of the Passover' in which they gave thanks to God for setting them free and because the Angel of Destruction did not harm them but 'passed over' them.

During their long journey through the wilderness to the Promised Land they were guided by pillars of cloud and of fire. The Egyptians pursued them but they were saved by the waters of the Sea of Reeds. They were fed by manna and quails from heaven and water gushed from rocks to quench their thirst.

Once, during their wanderings, Moses went up into a mountain to talk to God. There he was given the Ten Commandments. These were placed in a special container called the Ark of the Covenant and kept in a special Tent which was called the Tabernacle.

The Israelites finally reached the borders of the Promised Land and, with this in sight, Moses said good-bye to his people and climbed Mt. Nebo. There, quite alone, he died. Every year after that the people celebrated the Feast of the Passover.

FOR YOUR NOTEBOOK

1. Exodus is the second book of the Bible and it means 'going out' or 'departure'. Write the names of the first ten books of the Bible.
2. Read Exodus **14** and draw pictures to illustrate the story.
3. Read Exodus **20.** 1-17, and write the Ten Commandments in ten short sentences.

THE EXODUS

MANY PLAGUES CAME TO THE
EGYPTIANS AND PHARAOH LET
THE ISRAELITES GO
CANAAN
The Promised Land
Dead
Sea
GOSHEN
The Sea
of Reeds
EGYPT
QUAILS
MANNA
R. Nile
Mt. Sinai
THE TABERNACLE
THE 10 COMMANDMENTS

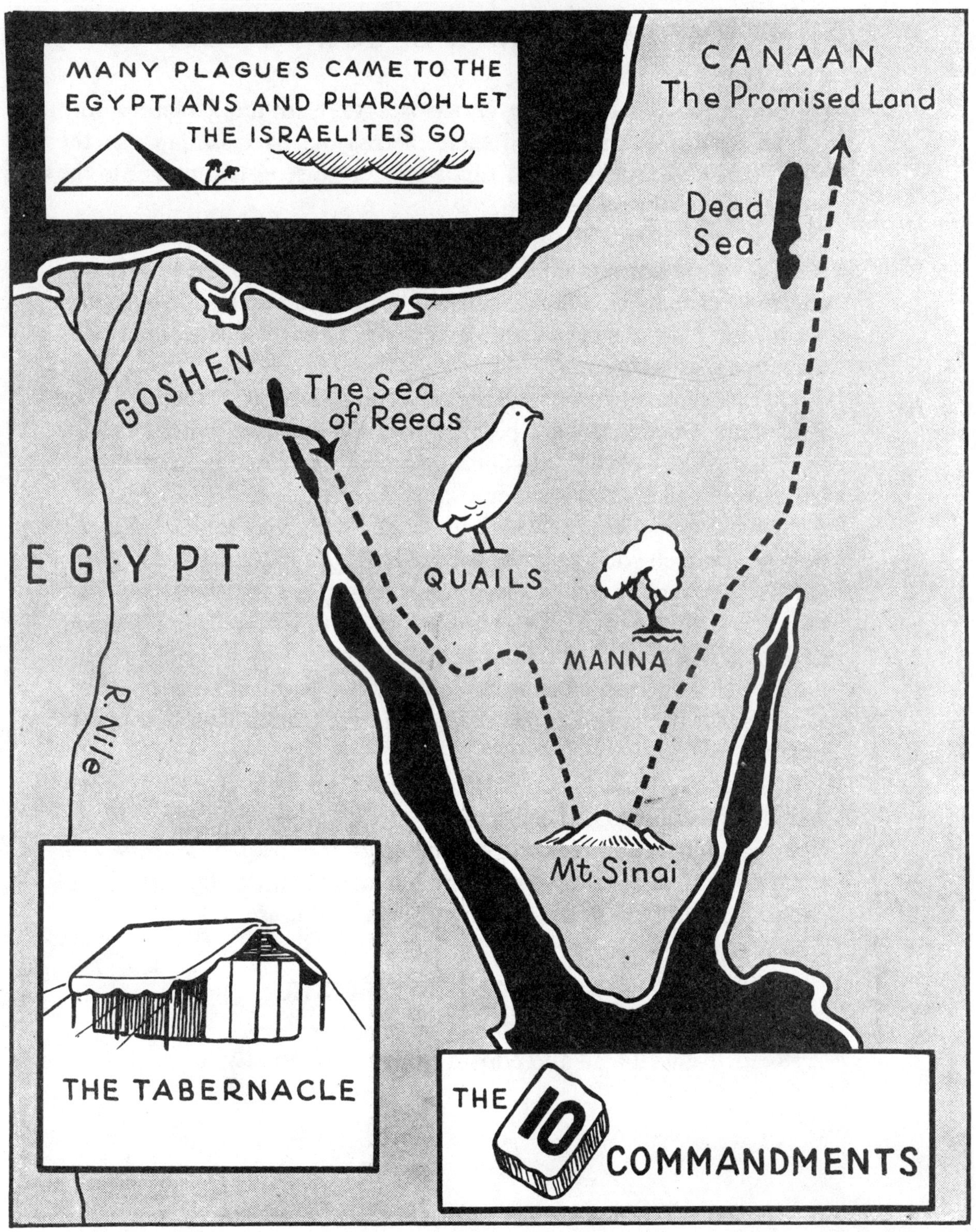

JOSHUA—THE WARRIOR LEADER

JOSHUA was chosen by Moses to lead the Israelites into Canaan. In front of them, across the river Jordan, lay the city of Jericho, and Joshua decided to send two men into the city to spy out the land.

They entered the city secretly and lodged with a woman named Rahab, whose house was on the city wall. When, later, they were discovered by the King's soldiers, Rahab helped them to escape by a cord let down from her window and they returned to Joshua to report that the city could be taken.

Then Joshua gave the command to cross the river Jordan. The Ark of the Covenant went before them and as they approached the river the waters parted. Joshua caused twelve stones, one for each tribe, to be set up as a memorial at this place.

Arriving outside the walls of Jericho, Joshua commanded his people to march round the walls once every day for six days. On the seventh day they marched seven times round the city, trumpets were blown and they raised a mighty shout. At this, the walls fell down and the city was entered and captured.

After this success, Joshua conquered many towns and gradually the Israelite tribes began to settle down with their Canaanite neighbours.

Joshua set up the Tabernacle or Tent of Meeting at Shiloh, where Abraham had his first encampment.

Before his death, Joshua commanded the people to serve the Lord faithfully. He took a great stone and set it up under an oak tree at Shechem to remind the Israelites of their promise to God.

FOR YOUR NOTEBOOK

1. Draw a picture to illustrate any part of the story.
2. Read Joshua **24.** 14 and copy it in your best handwriting.

JOSHUA

JOSHUA, THE SON OF NUN, LED THE ISRAELITES INTO CANAAN

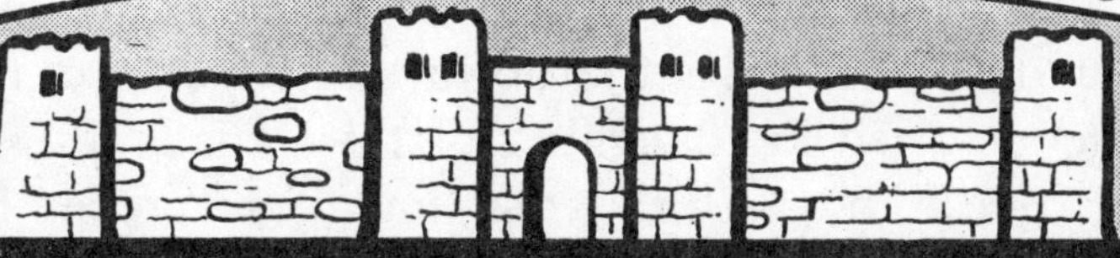

HE HAD TO CONQUER THE CITY OF JERICHO

SPIES WERE SENT INTO THE CITY

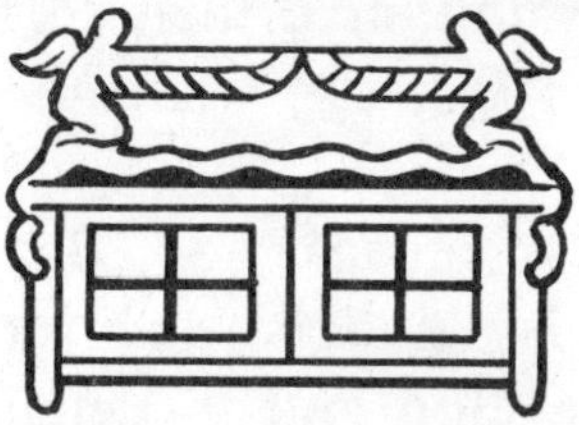

WITH THE ARK BEFORE THEM

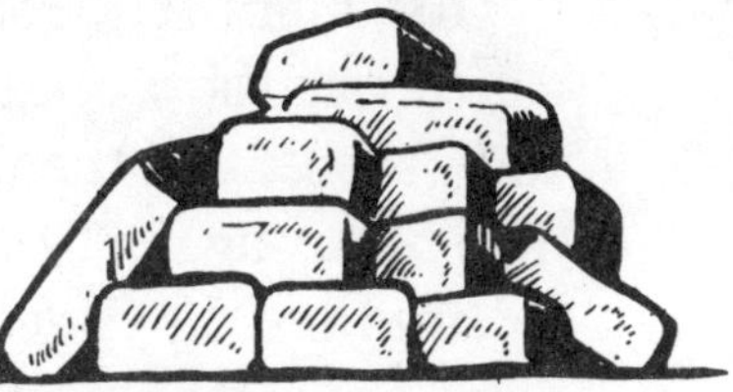

THE ISRAELITES CROSSED THE RIVER JORDAN

7 TIMES THEY MARCHED ROUND THE CITY

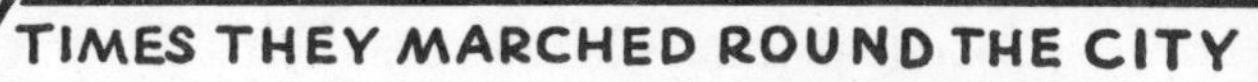

TRUMPETS WERE BLOWN

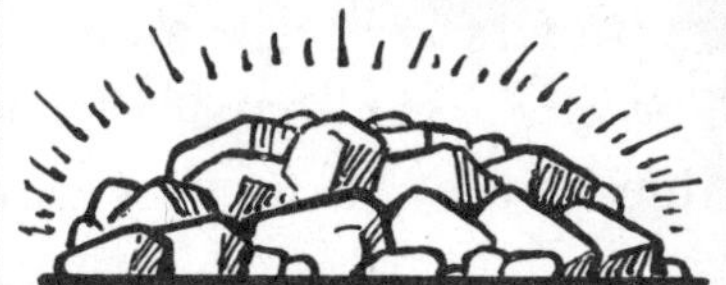

THE WALLS OF THE CITY COLLAPSED

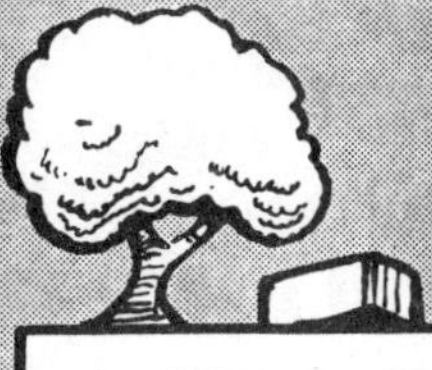

JOSHUA TAUGHT THE ISRAELITES

"Serve ye the Lord"

JOSHUA XXIV. 14

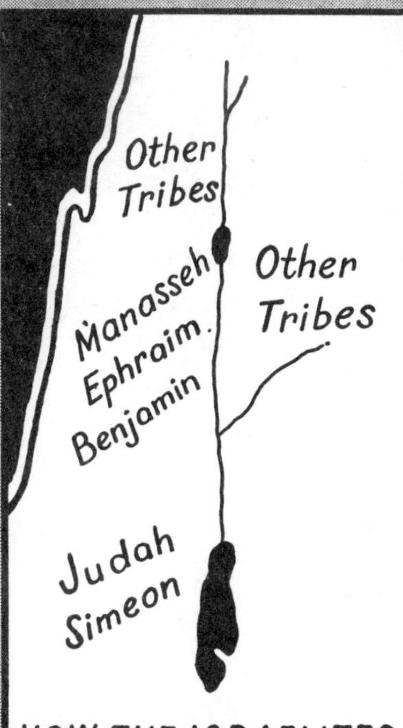

HOW THE ISRAELITES SETTLED IN CANAAN

GIDEON—ONE OF THE BRAVE JUDGES

THE Israelites no longer led a wandering life but began to build houses and settle down in villages. As time went by they married the daughters of the Canaanites and began to worship the local gods. During this time they were led by Judges or 'heroes' and one of the bravest of these was Gideon.

For many years the Israelites were attacked by desert tribes called Midianites (or Arabs) who raided their villages and stole their corn. One day, Gideon, who was threshing his corn secretly, was called by God to save the Israelites.

That night, Gideon cut down the tree pole of a local god, Baal, which was the wooden image that some of the Israelites worshipped, and called upon the people to return to the true God and to defend themselves against their enemies.

From 10,000 Gideon chose 300 of the most alert men by watching how they drank at a stream. He armed these men with a trumpet and a flaming torch concealed in a pitcher.

That night the Israelites surrounded the huge Midianite army and, at Gideon's command, smashed their pitchers and blew their trumpets. With a mighty shout of 'The sword of the Lord and of Gideon,' they advanced.

The Midianites, aroused from their sleep, thought that many armies were attacking and they fled in terror.

After this great victory the Israelites wanted Gideon to be king but he refused, saying 'The Lord shall rule over you'.

During the time of Gideon the Midianites never attacked again.

FOR YOUR NOTEBOOK

1. Read Judges **7.** 16-21, and write the story in your own words.
2. Draw and colour a picture of a flaming torch, a trumpet, and a banner with Gideon's war cry.
3. Further reading — Judges **6.** 11-16; 25-27, and **7.** 1-8.

GIDEON

THE TRIBES
WERE NOW
LED BY
JUDGES
THE ISRAELITES
WORSHIPPED
BAAL
ATTACKED
BY
DESERT
TRIBES
(Midianites)
WHILST
WINNOWING
GIDEON
IS CALLED
BY GOD
HE DESTROYS
THE LOCAL
GODS –
BAALS
300
MEN ARE CHOSEN
AT THE
STREAM
THEY
DESTROY THE
MIDIANITES
FOR
GOD
AND
GIDEON

SAMSON AND THE PHILISTINES

ALTHOUGH Samson was called a Judge he was not like the other Judges for he never led the Israelites into battle. Famous for his deeds of strength, he fought alone against the Philistines.

The Philistines were a new enemy. They came from an island in the Mediterranean called Crete and they settled on the coast of Canaan in the five cities of Ashdod, Ashkelon, Gaza, Ekron and Gath.

Samson lived in a village near Ekron. He was dedicated to God by his parents and, as a sign of this, he was forbidden to cut his hair.

Many stories are told of his great strength. He killed a lion with his bare hands and destroyed many Philistines with the jawbone of an ass. When they tried to imprison him in Gath he tore down the huge city gates and carried them away on his back.

In the end he was betrayed by his wife Delilah, who was herself a Philistine. She persuaded Samson to reveal the secret of his great strength which was supposed to lie in his long hair. Whilst he slept, Delilah cut his hair and then called the Philistine soldiers. Samson was captured and thrown into prison. There he was blinded and made to grind corn as a punishment.

The Philistines, to celebrate his capture, arranged a feast in the Temple of Dagon. Samson was brought out to be taunted. He asked to be placed between the two pillars which supported the roof and, praying to God for strength, he moved them so that the roof collapsed.

Samson was killed, but many Philistines also died that day.

FOR YOUR NOTEBOOK

1. Draw a map to show the five cities of the Philistines.
2. Read Judges **16.** 23-30 and draw a picture to illustrate the story.
3. Samson was fond of riddles. Write down some riddles that you know.

SAMSON

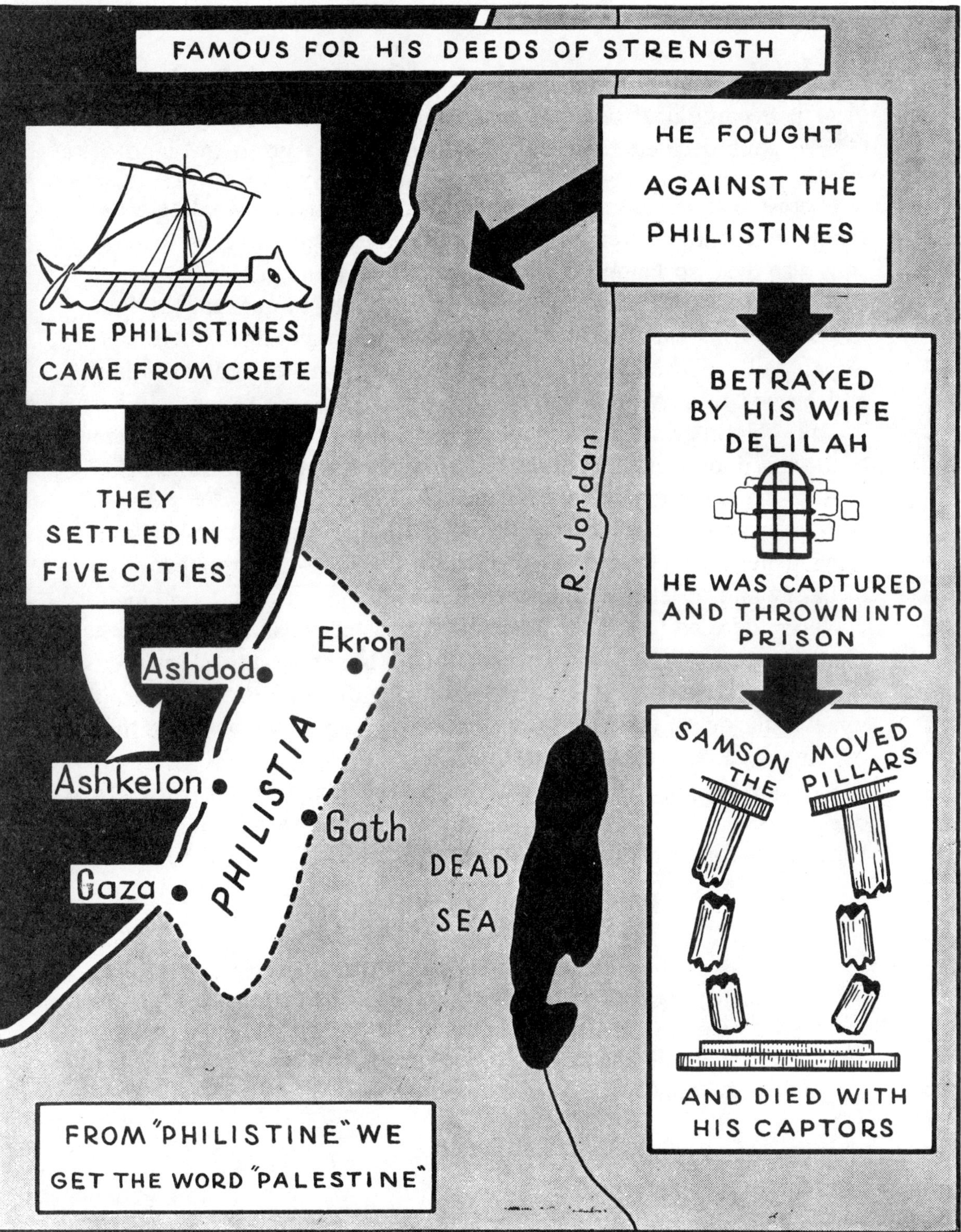

FAMOUS FOR HIS DEEDS OF STRENGTH
THE PHILISTINES CAME FROM CRETE
THEY SETTLED IN FIVE CITIES
Ashdod
Ekron
Ashkelon
Gath
Gaza
PHILISTIA
FROM "PHILISTINE" WE GET THE WORD "PALESTINE"
R. Jordan
DEAD SEA
HE FOUGHT AGAINST THE PHILISTINES
BETRAYED BY HIS WIFE DELILAH
HE WAS CAPTURED AND THROWN INTO PRISON
SAMSON MOVED THE PILLARS
AND DIED WITH HIS CAPTORS

RUTH THE FAITHFUL

IN the days of the Judges there was a great famine in Canaan. Because of this, Elimelech and his wife Naomi and their two sons decided to leave Bethlehem and to go to the land of Moab.

There the family settled and the two sons married Moabite girls, Orpah and Ruth. After some years Elimelech died and then the two sons also died, so Naomi decided to return to Canaan.

Orpah and Ruth started back with her, but Naomi realised that she was taking them to a foreign land and urged them to return. Orpah sadly obeyed, but Ruth refused to leave her mother-in-law and begged to go with her.

Thus Naomi and Ruth went on to Bethlehem together. They were both very poor and, in order to get food, Ruth gleaned in the fields of Boaz, a distant relative of Elimelech.

Boaz heard of the devotion of Ruth to her mother-in-law and showed her great kindness by telling his reapers to drop handfuls of barley and to let her share their meals.

Naomi decided to sell her land and, by Eastern custom, her nearest relative had the right to buy this and, also, to marry Ruth. However, the nearest relative gave up his claim in favour of Boaz. This was done by the act of taking off a shoe and handing it over as a sign that the right had been transferred.

So Boaz bought the property from Naomi and married Ruth. In due course a child was born, called Obed, whose son Jesse later became the father of David, the greatest of the kings of Israel.

FOR YOUR NOTEBOOK

1. Read and copy in your best handwriting the words of Ruth, 'Intreat me not to leave thee . . .' etc., in Ruth **1.** 16-17.
2. Draw a picture of Ruth gleaning in the barley field.
3. Write down all the names that you know of women of the Old Testament.

RUTH

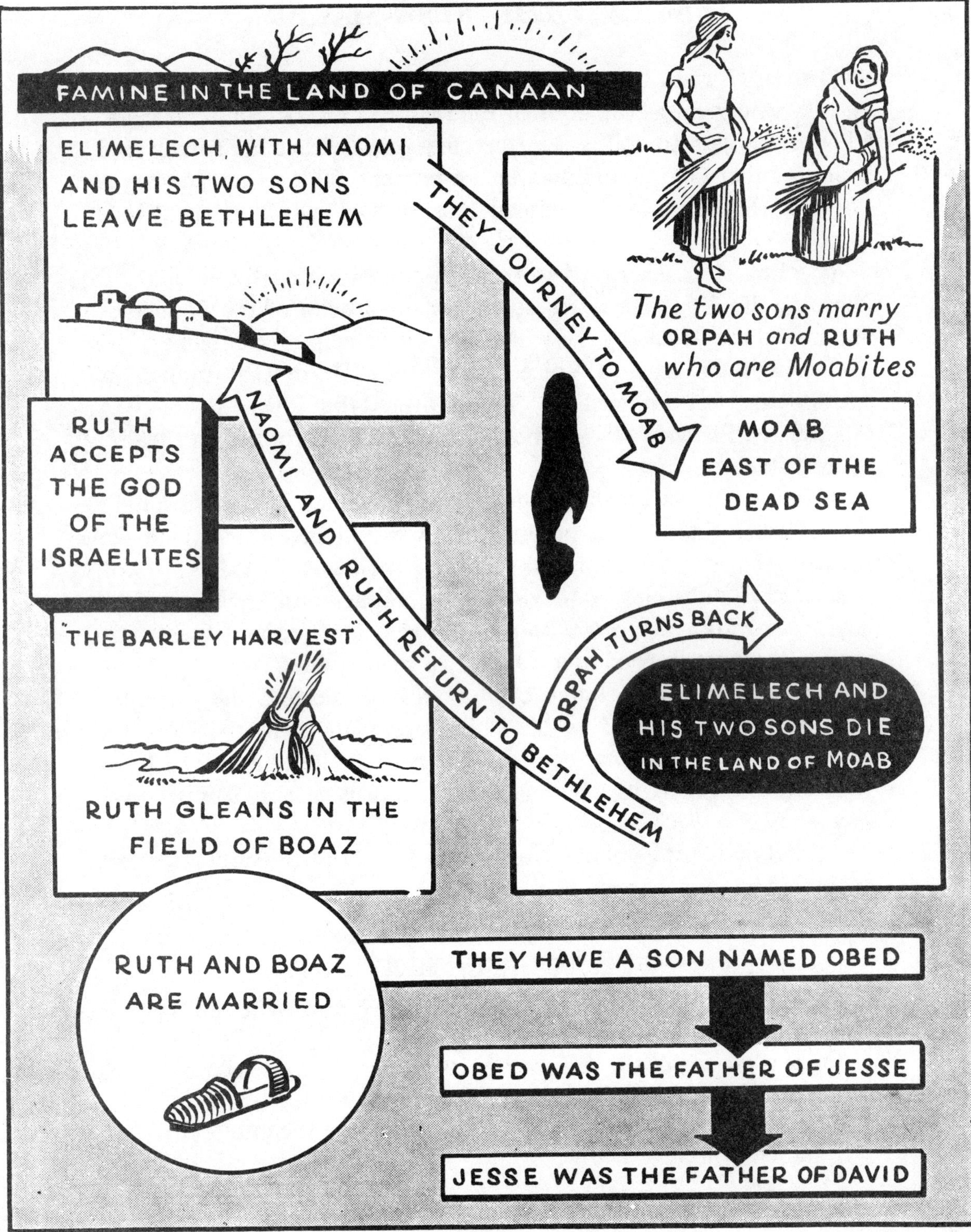

FAMINE IN THE LAND OF CANAAN
ELIMELECH, WITH NAOMI AND HIS TWO SONS LEAVE BETHLEHEM
THEY JOURNEY TO MOAB
The two sons marry ORPAH and RUTH who are Moabites
MOAB EAST OF THE DEAD SEA
RUTH ACCEPTS THE GOD OF THE ISRAELITES
NAOMI AND RUTH RETURN TO BETHLEHEM
ORPAH TURNS BACK
ELIMELECH AND HIS TWO SONS DIE IN THE LAND OF MOAB
"THE BARLEY HARVEST"
RUTH GLEANS IN THE FIELD OF BOAZ
RUTH AND BOAZ ARE MARRIED
THEY HAVE A SON NAMED OBED
OBED WAS THE FATHER OF JESSE
JESSE WAS THE FATHER OF DAVID

SAMUEL THE KING-MAKER

THERE was once a woman named Hannah, the wife of Elkanah who wept at the door of the House of God in Shiloh because she had no child. Eli, the chief priest, heard her sorrow and promised that God would answer her prayer. In due time a son was born to Hannah and she named him Samuel which means 'God-given'.

As a boy, Samuel served in the Temple, trimming the lamps and guarding the Ark. He heard stories of the cruelty of the Philistines and hoped that, one day, he would be able to help his people.

One night he heard a Voice calling him. At first he thought it was Eli but, after the third time, he discovered that it was the Voice of God. Then Eli knew that Samuel was to be the prophet and leader of the Israelites.

During a battle with the Philistines the Israelites foolishly brought the Ark into their camp, hoping that it would save them from the enemy. The Ark was captured and the Israelites defeated.

Now the Philistines were visited by plagues and, seven months later, they returned the Ark thinking that it had brought them only trouble. It was returned in a cart drawn by unguided oxen.

Samuel was made a judge over all his people and the Israelites were no longer troubled by the Philistines. However, the Israelites once again wanted a king. Samuel at first refused, saying, "The Lord your God is your King', but the Israelites insisted and Samuel gave way.

Guided by God, he chose Saul whom he met at the city gates and anointed him with oil as king over Israel.

FOR YOUR NOTEBOOK

1. Read the Call of Samuel in I Samuel **3.** 2-9, and write the story in your own words.
2. Draw a picture of the Ark being returned in a cart drawn by oxen, or make a model of this in cardboard and Plasticine.
3. Samuel means 'God-given' — write down the meanings of other names you have learnt.

SAMUEL

SON OF HANNAH AND ELKANAH

AS A BOY HE SERVES IN THE TEMPLE

HE HEARS THE WORD OF GOD

AND BECOMES A LEADER OF A NATION

ISRAEL IS TROUBLED BY THE PHILISTINES

THEY CAPTURE THE ARK

AFTER SEVEN MONTHS

THE ARK IS RETURNED

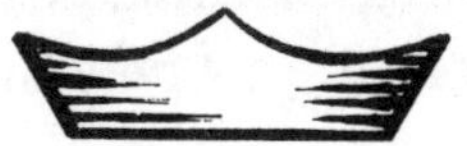

THE PEOPLE ASK FOR A KING TO LEAD THEM AGAINST THE PHILISTINES

SAMUEL MEETS SAUL THE SON OF KISH AT THE CITY GATES

SAMUEL ANOINTS SAUL AS KING

SAUL—FIRST KING OF ISRAEL

SAUL was chosen to be king not because he was wise and fitted to rule, but because he was big and handsome and a brave warrior.

Soon after he was made king, the Ammonites attacked the city of Jabesh-gilead. Saul cleverly attacked them from three sides at once and completely defeated them. This victory made him very popular.

Saul now turned his attention to defeating the Philistines who had invaded the country. His son, Jonathan, struck the first blow at Gibeah (where the Philistines had a stronghold) by killing their general and driving the enemy back. The Philistine army then attacked in force and Saul and Jonathan had to fall back on Gibeah.

One night, with great bravery, Jonathan and his armour bearer stole up on the Philistine sentries and, in a narrow ravine, killed them one by one. This caused a panic and, as an earthquake followed, the Philistines fled in terror.

Some years later Saul defeated the Amalekites, who were a desert tribe, but he disobeyed God's command and Samuel looked for another king. He found David, the son of Jesse, at Bethlehem and anointed him as Israel's new king.

David became the armour bearer to Saul and soothed his fits of depression by playing the harp.

FOR YOUR NOTEBOOK

1. Read how Saul was anointed king — I Samuel **9.** 25 to **10.** **1.**
2. Read about the Ammonites in I Samuel **11.** 11-15 and write the story in your own words.
3. Read about Jonathan's adventure in I Samuel **14.** 11-23 and draw Jonathan and his armour bearer.

SAUL

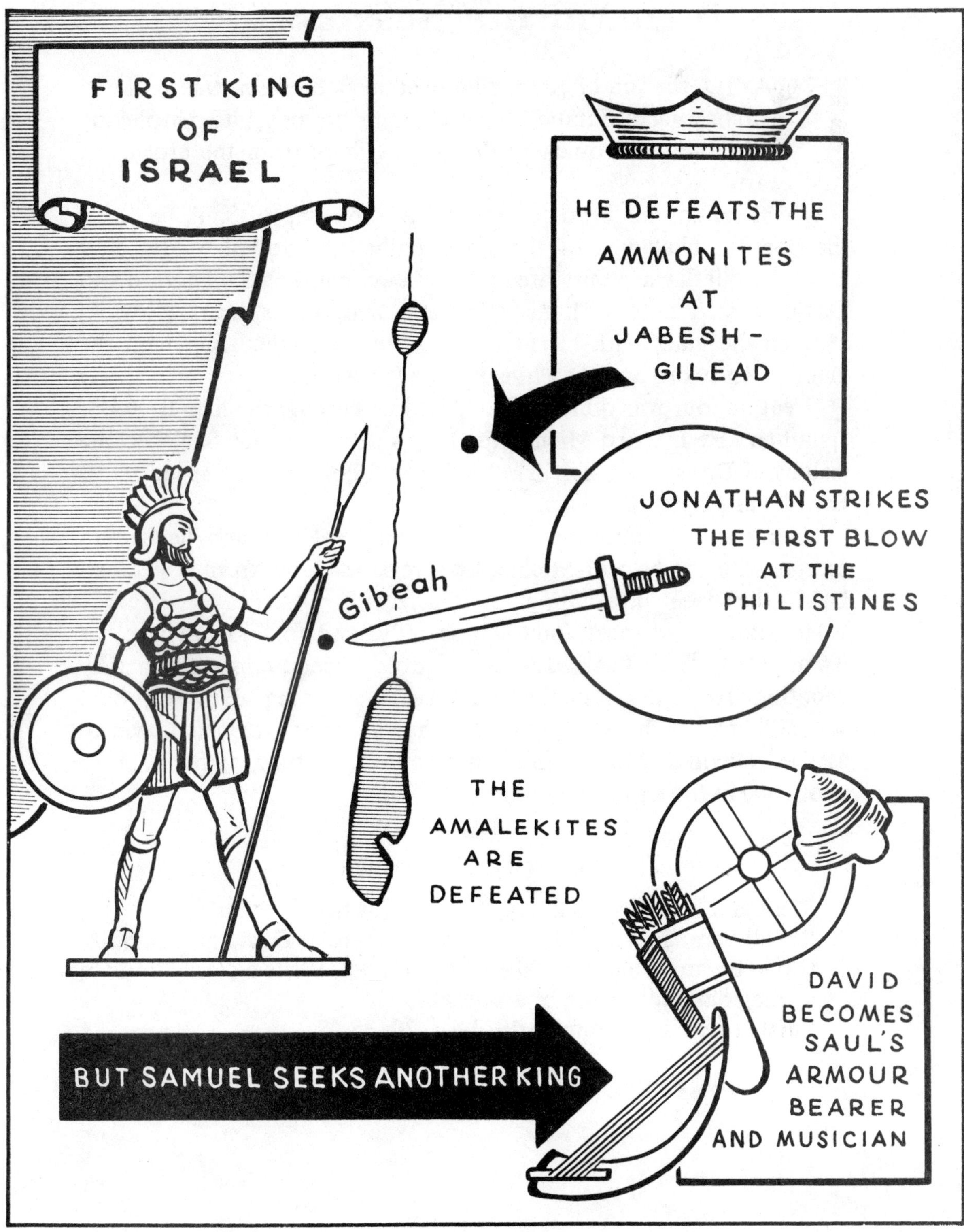
FIRST KING OF ISRAEL
HE DEFEATS THE AMMONITES AT JABESH-GILEAD
JONATHAN STRIKES THE FIRST BLOW AT THE PHILISTINES
Gibeah
THE AMALEKITES ARE DEFEATED
DAVID BECOMES SAUL'S ARMOUR BEARER AND MUSICIAN
BUT SAMUEL SEEKS ANOTHER KING

DAVID THE SHEPHERD

DAVID, the son of Jesse, who lived in Bethlehem, was anointed to be king by Samuel. He was a shepherd boy, gifted in playing the harp and quick to defend his flock from the attacks of wild beasts.

Whilst visiting his brothers one day at the camp of Saul, he heard the boastful challenge of the giant Philistine, Goliath. His offer to fight Goliath was at first treated as a joke, but then Saul agreed and David, armed only with his sling and five stones from a brook, stunned the giant with his first shot. He then killed him with the giant's own sword and the Philistines fled in terror.

Great honour was done to David and he became the firm friend of Jonathan. He married Michal, the king's daughter, but Saul became jealous of David's success. He tried to kill him with his spear whilst David was playing the harp.

Then David's house was surrounded by soldiers and he had to escape, with the help of Michal, by a rope let down from a window. David then went into hiding.

He returned to meet Jonathan secretly, and to find out whether it was safe to come back. Jonathan agreed to send him a message by shooting arrows into a field where David was hiding. However, Saul was still mad with anger, and Jonathan's arrows warned David to escape. David fled for his life and became an outlaw, with a band of about 400 in the Cave of Adullam.

FOR YOUR NOTEBOOK

1. Read and learn Psalm **23** — 'The Lord is my Shepherd'.
2. Read I Samuel **17.** 37-51, and draw a picture of David and Goliath.
3. David became an outlaw like Robin Hood. Write a story about an imaginary adventure of an outlaw.
4. Further reading: I Samuel **19.** 1-12; **20.** 35-42.

DAVID

SON OF JESSE
BETHLEHEM
HE IS A SHEPHERD
ANOINTED BY SAMUEL TO BE KING
HE SLAYS THE GIANT GOLIATH
BEFRIENDED BY JONATHAN
DAVID MARRIES MICHAL DAUGHTER OF SAUL
SAUL BECOMES THE ENEMY OF DAVID
HELPED BY MICHAL, DAVID ESCAPES
HE HIDES IN A FIELD
AND IS WARNED BY JONATHAN'S ARROWS
THE CAVE OF ADULLAM
DAVID FLEES AND BECOMES AN OUTLAW

DAVID THE KING

WHEN David became an outlaw he first sought refuge with the Philistines. During this time the Philistines thought that he was helping them, but David was really fighting against the desert tribes who were enemies of the Israelites.

Whilst David was attacking the desert tribes, the Philistines marched against the Israelites and utterly defeated them. Jonathan was killed and Saul died by his own hand.

With the death of Saul, the people of Judah chose David to be their king and, later, the tribes of Israel joined them. Now David ruled over a united people.

Jerusalem, an old mountain fortress held by the Jebusites, lay mid-way between the northern and southern parts of the kingdom and David determined to make it his capital. The Jebusites mocked David, thinking that their fortress was too strong to be overcome. But David knew of a tunnel that lay beneath the city. He offered a great reward to anyone who would enter by this tunnel, and Joab led the way. He captured the city and David made Jerusalem his capital.

The Philistines now became alarmed at David's great power and they attacked in force. They were utterly defeated.

In spite of David's great victories he had many troubles. His favourite son, Absalom, rebelled. There was a battle in the forest of Ephraim, and Absalom, whilst trying to escape on his mule, became entangled in the branches of an oak. Joab put him to death and when David was told he was overcome with grief.

After this victory all Israel was united again under the shield of David. Before he died, David had Solomon, his son, anointed king over all Israel.

FOR YOUR NOTEBOOK

1. Read Psalm **24** — a Psalm of David — and learn verses 3-6.
2. Draw a picture of a fortress and, in a few sentences, explain how Jerusalem was captured.
3. Draw and colour a crown and banner with the words, 'David — King of Judah and Israel'.

DAVID

DAVID MAKES FRIENDS WITH THE PHILISTINES
MT. GILBOA
JONATHAN AND SAUL ARE SLAIN
DAVID BECOMES KING OF JUDAH AND UNITES JUDAH WITH ISRAEL
ISRAEL
JUDAH
DAVID CAPTURES JERUSALEM
The Star of David
THE PHILISTINES ARE DEFEATED
HIS SON ABSALOM REBELS AND IS SLAIN BY JOAB
DAVID CHOOSES SOLOMON TO BE KING

SOLOMON IN ALL HIS GLORY

SOLOMON became king after David when the country was united and at peace. During his reign the kingdom developed in power and prosperity. By marrying an Egyptian princess he strengthened his hold on the trade routes and he made many treaties with the nations around him.

As time went on the wisdom of Solomon was recognised and he was famous for his wise sayings, proverbs and riddles.

By an agreement with the seafaring Phoenicians he traded westwards and, helped by the king of Tyre, he built his own merchant fleet. His ships traded between many countries bringing precious cargoes of spices, sandalwood, ivory and gold.

Solomon determined to build, in Jerusalem, a magnificent temple to God. It was oblong in shape with three main parts — the Entrance Porch, the Holy Place, and the Holy of Holies where the Ark was placed. Its outer walls were of white marble.

Inside, the walls were lined with cedar wood and covered with gold. Two huge pillars guarded the entrance, and the temple was completed after seven years of toil.

But all this magnificence meant heavy taxes, and just before Solomon died Israel was at the point of revolution.

When Solomon died in 930 B.C., his son Rehoboam became king. He refused to listen to the demands for less taxation and Jeroboam, who had been a leader of Solomon's workmen, led a rebellion against him.

Soon the whole nation was split in two. The south was for Rehoboam and the north made Jeroboam their king.

FOR YOUR NOTEBOOK

1. Draw and colour a plan of Solomon's temple.
2. Read I Kings 7. 48-50, and make a list of the vessels in the temple.
3. Draw one of Solomon's ships.

SOLOMON

LAST KING OF JUDAH AND ISRAEL
N
W
E
S
Table of Shewbread
THE MOST HOLY PLACE
Ark
HOLY PLACE
PORCH
Plan of Solomon's Temple
SOLOMON MARRIES A DAUGHTER OF PHARAOH
HE BUILDS A MERCHANT NAVY
The Kingdom of Solomon
HEAVY TAXES LEAD TO REBELLION
THE NORTHERN TRIBES REBEL
JEROBOAM v. REHOBOAM

ELIJAH—THE FIERY PROPHET

ABOUT fifty years after Israel was divided, Ahab came to the throne. His queen was Jezebel, the daughter of the king of the Sidonians, and she encouraged the king to worship Baal.

To the east of Jordan, in the mountains of Gilead, there lived a man named Elijah. He saw the wickedness of the people of Israel and he suddenly appeared before Ahab. He warned the king that, as a punishment, drought and famine would come to the land.

Elijah's threat put his life in danger and he was warned by God to go to the brook Cherith where the ravens fed him.

After a while even Cherith had no water and Elijah went to Zarephath. There he met a widow, gathering sticks, and he asked her for food. He promised that God would care for her and, whilst the drought lasted, her barrel of meal and cruse of oil were never empty.

For three years Ahab had searched for Elijah and now the prophet revealed himself. He proposed to the king that there should be a contest between him and the prophets of Baal. There gathered on Mount Carmel four hundred and fifty priests of Baal and one man of God, Elijah.

There were two bullocks for sacrifice. The priests chose one and placing it on an altar called to their god to send down fire to consume it — but nothing came. Then Elijah built up his altar, put another bullock on it, and soaked it all with water. Then he prayed to God, and fire fell and burnt up everything.

The prophets of Baal were put to death and the drought came to an end.

Elijah went up by a whirlwind into heaven, and his prophet's mantle was worn by Elisha, who succeeded him.

FOR YOUR NOTEBOOK

1. Read I Kings **17.** 1-7, and draw a picture of Elijah being fed by the ravens.
2. Read I Kings **17.** 8-16.
3. Read I Kings **18.** 17 to the end. Write the story of the contest between Elijah and the priests of Baal in your own words.

ELIJAH

ELIJAH, THE HERMIT WARNS THE WORSHIPPERS OF BAAL
As the Lord God of Israel liveth, there shall not be dew nor rain these years
AHAB
AND
JEZEBEL
He is fed by the ravens
ELIJAH GOES
TO THE BROOK CHERITH
THE BROOK DRIES UP
ZAREPHATH
HE IS FED BY THE WIDOW
THE DROUGHT IS BROKEN
Mount Carmel
ELIJAH RETURNS AND CHALLENGES THE PROPHETS OF BAAL
THE MANTLE OF ELIJAH FALLS UPON ELISHA

ELISHA—MAN OF GOD

ELIJAH placed his sheepskin mantle over the shoulders of Elisha as a sign that Elisha was his successor. When Elijah was taken up to heaven in a whirlwind, Elisha was recognised by the prophets as their leader.

Elisha did many acts of kindness. A widow was in great debt — all she had was a pot of oil. He told her to gather all the vessels that she could and to fill them from the pot of oil. This she did and was able to sell the oil to pay off her debt. He restored to life the son of the lady of Shunem, who had died of sunstroke, and he cured Naaman, the Syrian general, of his leprosy by commanding him to bathe in the Jordan.

The king of Syria made plans to attack the Israelites by surprise but always his plans were known. He blamed Elisha for this and planned to capture him at Dothan. As the Syrians surrounded Dothan they were struck with blindness. Elisha led them into Samaria, the heart of Israel, and their eyes were opened.

Again the Syrians attacked. They surrounded the city of Samaria and began the long siege. Food grew very scarce but Elisha promised that relief would come. That night four lepers, who lived outside the city, went into the camp of the Syrians. They found the camp deserted and carried back the news. So Elisha's prophecy came true, and there was food in plenty once again.

When Elisha lay dying he told king Jehoash to shoot an arrow towards Damascus so that he would remember to remain loyal to God and to smite the Syrians.

FOR YOUR NOTEBOOK

1. Read 2 Kings **4.** 1-7 and draw a picture of the widow, filling the vessels of oil. Write the story in your own words.
2. Further reading:
   2 Kings **7.** 3-16 — The Flight of the Syrians.
   2 Kings **13.** 14-19 — The Death of Elisha.

ELISHA

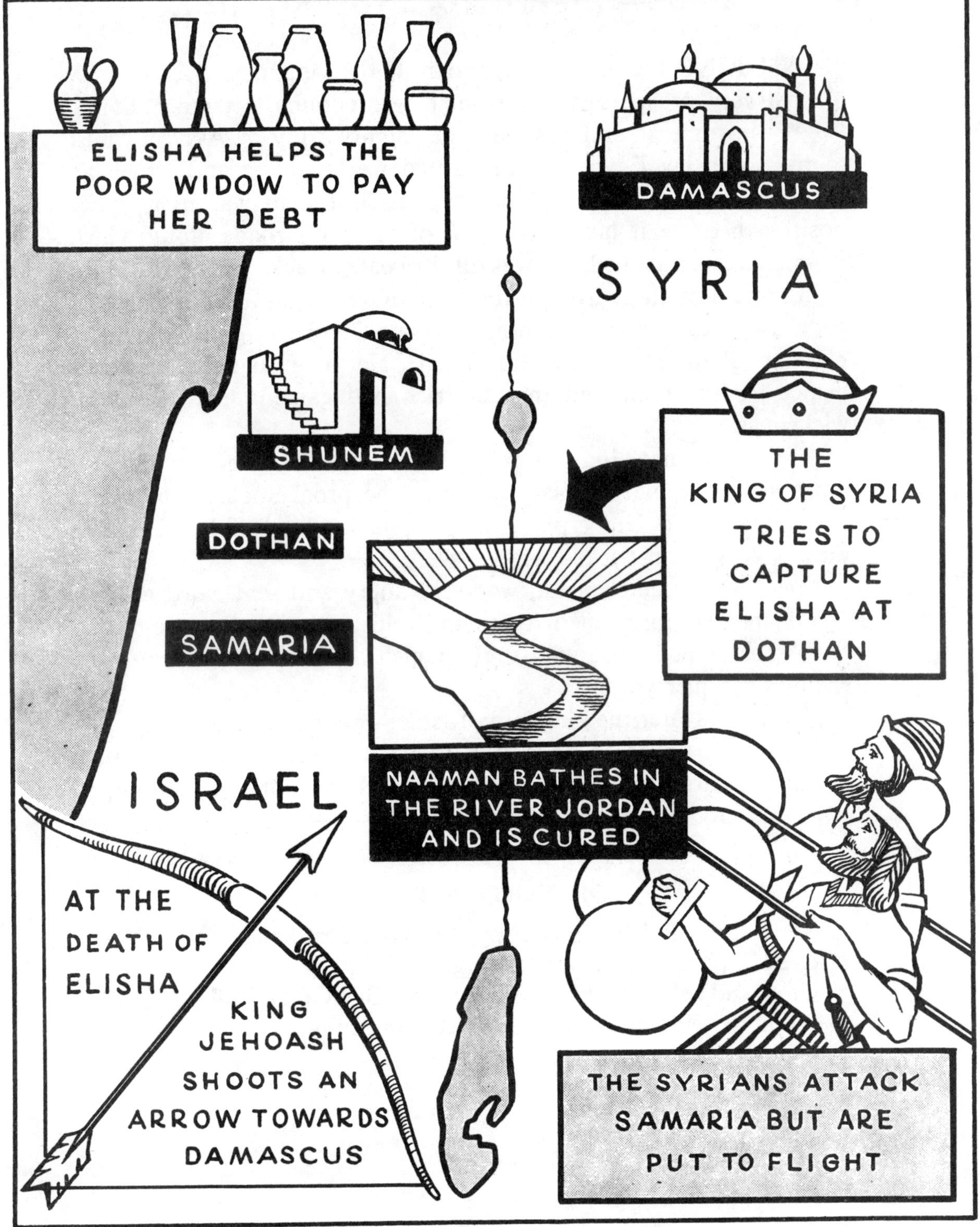

ELISHA HELPS THE POOR WIDOW TO PAY HER DEBT
DAMASCUS
SYRIA
SHUNEM
THE KING OF SYRIA TRIES TO CAPTURE ELISHA AT DOTHAN
DOTHAN
SAMARIA
ISRAEL
NAAMAN BATHES IN THE RIVER JORDAN AND IS CURED
AT THE DEATH OF ELISHA
KING JEHOASH SHOOTS AN ARROW TOWARDS DAMASCUS
THE SYRIANS ATTACK SAMARIA BUT ARE PUT TO FLIGHT

AMOS—SHEPHERD AND PROPHET

DURING the reign of Jeroboam II the kingdom of Israel grew very prosperous but trouble was coming to them. To the north east and east lay the mighty army of Assyria whilst to the south lay Egypt. Both wanted world power and Israel lay between them. Judah and her capital Jerusalem was in a better position because it lay to the east of the busy roads along which the merchants travelled and was off the beaten track.

In those days there lived in the town of Tekoa, in the wilderness of Judah, a herdsman called Amos. He saw the cheating in the market places of Bethel, Samaria, and Gilgal. He knew that there was no justice for the poor and that the rich had gained their power by wickedness.

Amos knew that God was calling him to speak out boldly and one morning in the market place at Bethel he proclaimed his message. Amos threatened God's punishment upon the land of Israel if they did not cease their wicked ways.

Amaziah, the chief priest, was very angry and sent word to king Jeroboam. He threatened Amos and told him to go back to Judah but Amos replied 'God will surely punish the people by letting your enemies conquer you'.

Many years later the kingdom of Israel went down as a nation.

Amos only appeared once at Bethel but he left a written record. He was the first person to preach that God was not just the God of Israel but God of all the earth.

FOR YOUR NOTEBOOK

1. Read Amos 5. 24-27 and copy it in your best handwriting.
2. Draw a picture of Amos tending his sheep.
3. Draw and colour a flag with the words 'One God for all the World,' and write down the names of as many countries as you can.

AMOS

The Great Sea
ASSYRIA
SYRIA
ISRAEL
788 B.C.
Tekoa
JUDAH
EGYPT
ASSYRIA THREATENS THE SMALLER STATES
AMOS SPEAKS OUT AGAINST THE EVIL IN ISRAEL
ONE GOD FOR ALL THE WORLD
N
W
E
S
AMOS SHEPHERD AND PROPHET

ISAIAH—STATESMAN AND PROPHET

THREE hundred years after David, the kingdom of Judah was prosperous under King Uzziah. In Jerusalem a boy was born called Isaiah. His parents were wealthy and Isaiah became a friend of the king.

As a boy he had listened to the words of Amos and he saw that the people had forgotten their God. Assyria was beginning to move westwards and danger threatened.

Isaiah had a vision from God and knew that he must warn the people of their danger. He tried many ways. One was the Parable of the Vineyard in which he compared the people of Judah with an unfruitful vineyard that would be trodden down.

Then Uzziah died and Ahaz came to the throne. Syria joined forces with Israel against Judah, and King Ahaz foolishly sought the help of Assyria by offering them gold and silver from the Temple.

Again Isaiah tried to warn the king. He made a large clay tablet, like a poster, with the words MAHER — SHALAL — HASH — BAZ and set it up in the market place. It was a terrible warning to the nation of their danger.

When Ahaz died Hezekiah became king. He rebelled against Assyria by seeking the aid of Egypt. The king of Assyria, who had already carried away the ten tribes of Israel, now marched upon Jerusalem. Hezekiah turned to Isaiah for help and the prophet told him to clear away the idols and turn again to God. This was done and the Assyrian army vanished and its camp lay empty.

Isaiah looked forward to the day in which God would send a king who would rule righteously. Christians looking back on Isaiah's words 'For unto us a child is born, unto us a son is given' claim that Jesus fulfilled the prophet's vision.

FOR YOUR NOTEBOOK

1. Read the Parable of the Vineyard — Isaiah **5.** 1-18.
2. Draw and colour a poster with the words 'swift — spoil — speedy — prey'.
3. Read and learn Isaiah **40.** 1-5.

ISAIAH

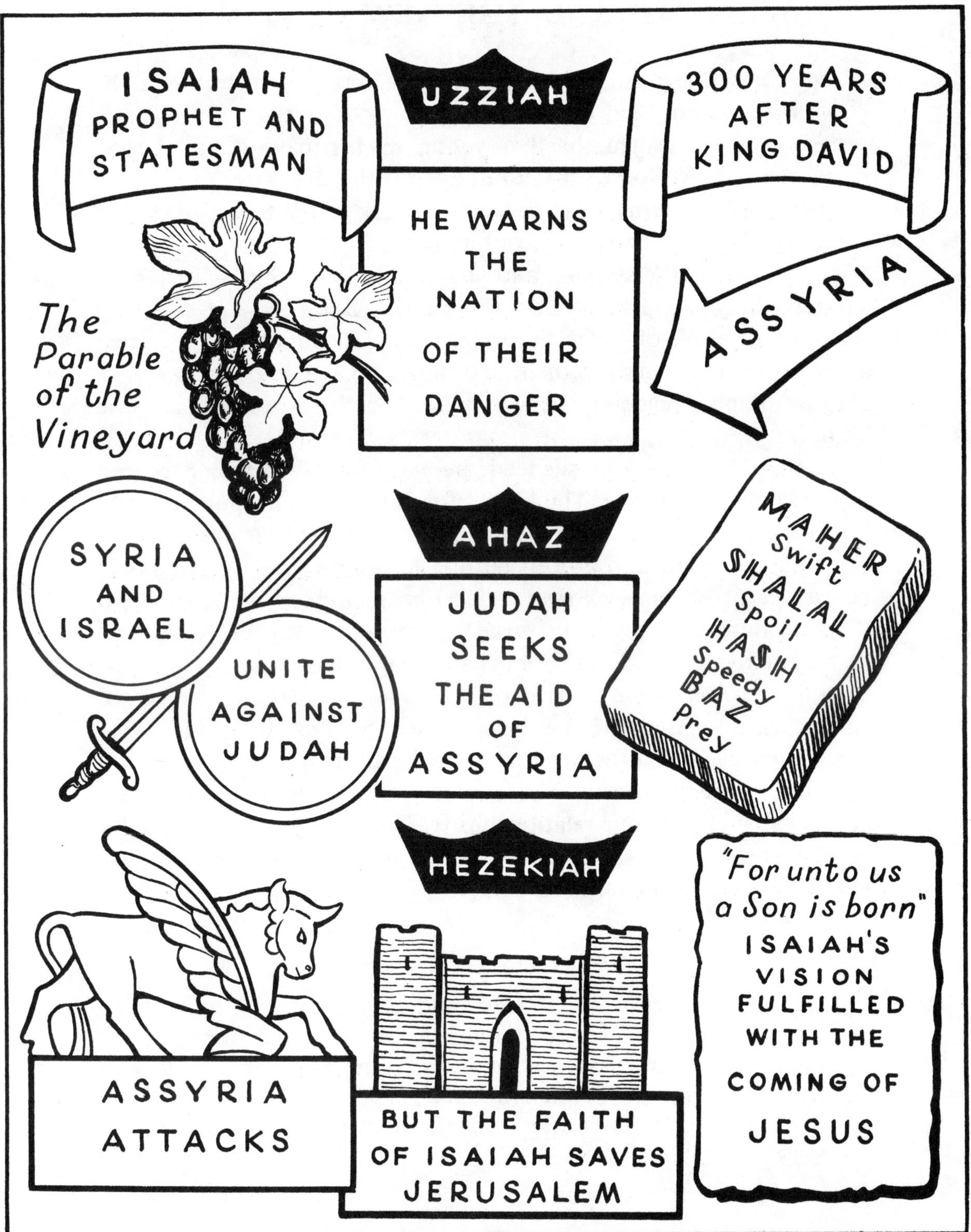

ISAIAH
PROPHET AND
STATESMAN
UZZIAH
300 YEARS
AFTER
KING DAVID
HE WARNS
THE
NATION
OF THEIR
DANGER
ASSYRIA
The
Parable
of the
Vineyard
AHAZ
SYRIA
AND
ISRAEL
UNITE
AGAINST
JUDAH
JUDAH
SEEKS
THE AID
OF
ASSYRIA
MAHER
Swift
SHALAL
Spoil
HASH
Speedy
BAZ
Prey
HEZEKIAH
ASSYRIA
ATTACKS
BUT THE FAITH
OF ISAIAH SAVES
JERUSALEM
"For unto us
a Son is born"
ISAIAH'S
VISION
FULFILLED
WITH THE
COMING OF
JESUS

JEREMIAH AND THE NEW COVENANT

AFTER the death of king Hezekiah, altars were built for the worship of Baal, and the true God was forgotten. In Anathoth, near Jerusalem, lived a young man named Jeremiah and he was chosen by God to speak out against this evil.

At first he was afraid, but he saw the work of the true God in the wonders of Nature and this gave him courage.

The powerful Assyrians and Egyptians had themselves been conquered by Nebuchadrezzar, the king of Babylon, and Jeremiah warned the people of Judah that their turn was coming. He smashed an earthenware jar to show them that they, also, would be broken and, because of his preaching, he was placed in the stocks outside the Temple.

Jeremiah refused to be silenced; he was accused of treachery and thrown into a dungeon. The king refused to have him put to death, but being a weak man, he gave him into the hands of the chief priests. They put Jeremiah into a deep pit and left him to die. Fortunately he was rescued by a black man called Ebedmelech.

Jeremiah's prophecy came true. Jerusalem was captured and destroyed by the army of Nebuchadrezzar. The king and princes and many people were carried off as slaves. Jeremiah was spared and returned to Anathoth, but he continued his work for God.

He saw clearly that the one real hope for all time was to make God a personal friend — write his Law in your hearts. This was an entirely new idea of our relationship to God. Jeremiah visualised a new covenant which Christians believe was fulfilled when God gave His Holy Spirit to all believers.

FOR YOUR NOTEBOOK

1. Draw a picture of a tree, flowers and birds and write the caption 'In the work of Nature, Jeremiah saw the hand of God'.
2. Read Jeremiah **38.** 7-13, and write in your own words how Jeremiah was rescued by the Ethiopian.
3. Design and colour a banner with the words 'God is a Friend'.

JEREMIAH

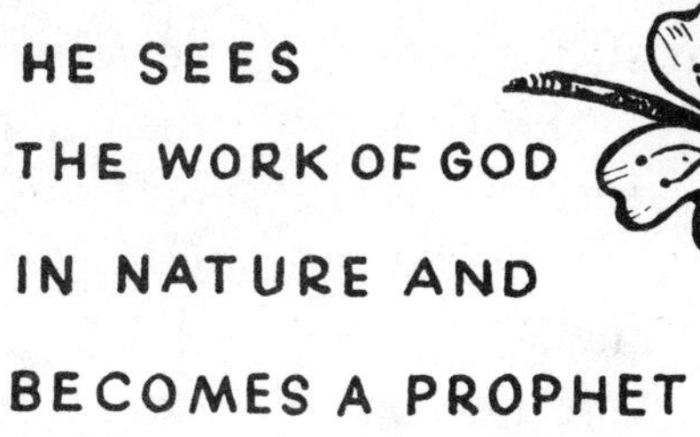

HE SEES THE WORK OF GOD IN NATURE AND BECOMES A PROPHET

HEATHEN GODS ARE WORSHIPPED IN JUDAH

JEREMIAH FORETELLS THAT JERUSALEM WILL BE BROKEN

JEREMIAH IS THROWN INTO A DUNGEON

FOR THAT HE IS PLACED IN THE STOCKS

EBED-MELECH RESCUES HIM FROM THE PIT

NEBUCHADREZZAR BESIEGES JERUSALEM

JERUSALEM IS DESTROYED BY THE ARMY OF BABYLON

THE NEW COVENANT

Write his Law in your hearts

JER. 31.31-34

DANIEL AND THE LIONS

IN the second century before Christ, the Jews were persecuted by Antiochus IV, king of Syria. During this time, many stories of old heroes were told secretly by the Jews to help them in their suffering and it is from these secret writings that we learn about a hero and prophet called Daniel.

One story tells us that four youths were chosen to serve at the Babylonian court — Shadrach, Meshach, Abed-nego and Daniel. Because Daniel could explain the meaning of dreams he was favoured and given great power.

Whilst Daniel was away, the emperor caused a golden image to be set up and called everyone to worship it, but Shadrach, Meshach, and Abed-nego refused. For this they were cast into a fiery furnace, but God was with them and they were unharmed.

Another story tells us that a foolish Gentile emperor gave a feast for a thousand of his lords. For the wine he used the sacred golden vessels from the Temple. As they drank and offered praises to their gods a hand appeared and wrote on the wall these words 'MENE-MENE-TEKEL-PERES'.

The emperor was greatly troubled and called Daniel to explain the meaning. Daniel explained 'God hath numbered thy kingdom and finished it'. That night the emperor was slain and another ruled in his place.

Finally there is this sequel. The nobles became jealous of Daniel and persuaded the king to make a law that no prayers should be offered to anyone — except to the king himself. Those who disobeyed were to be thrown into a den of lions.

Daniel was unafraid and continued to pray to God, in full view, by his open window. He was seized and thrown to the lions. But, next day, he was found to be unharmed for, because Daniel was not afraid to do right, God had protected him.

FOR YOUR NOTEBOOK

1. Read Daniel **3.** 19-27 — 'The Fiery Furnace'.
2. Draw an open window and write your own prayer by the side.
3. Read Daniel **6.** 4-23 — 'The Den of Lions'. Write the story in your own words, or draw a picture to illustrate this.

DANIEL

150 B.C.
ANTIOCHUS
SECRET WRITINGS FORM THE BOOK OF DANIEL
THE JEWS ARE PERSECUTED
SHADRACH
MESHACH
ABED-NEGO
THE FEAST OF THE FOOLISH EMPEROR
MENE MENE
TEKEL
PERES
God hath numbered thy kingdom and finished it
DANIEL PRAYS BY THE OPEN WINDOW
DANIEL IS SAVED FROM THE DEN OF LIONS